MATT CHRISTOPHER®

The #1 sports series for kids

★ LEGENDS IN SPORTS ★

BABE RUTH

Text by Glenn Stout

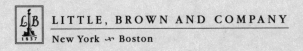

LITTLE, BROWN AND COMPANY
New York ⋅ Boston

Little, Brown and Company

Time Warner Book Group
1271 Avenue of the Americas, New York, NY 10020
Visit our Web site at www.lb-kids.com

www.mattchristopher.com

First Edition: September 2005

Matt Christopher® is a registered trademark of
Matt Christopher Royalties, Inc.

Text by Glenn Stout

Library of Congress Cataloging-in-Publication Data

Stout, Glenn, 1958–
    Babe Ruth / Matt Christopher ; [text by Glenn Stout]. — 1st ed.
        p.   cm. — (Legends in sports)
    ISBN 0-316-01113-4
    1. Ruth, Babe, 1895–1948 — Juvenile literature.   2. Baseball players —
United States — Biography — Juvenile literature.   I. Christopher, Matt.
II. Title.   III. Series.

GV865.R8S76   2005
796.357'092—dc22   2005007978

10 9 8 7 6 5 4 3 2 1

COM-MO

Printed in the United States of America

Contents

★ CHAPTER ONE ★

1895–1914

From the Street to St. Mary's

A teammate of Babe Ruth once said, "I saw a man transformed from a human being into something pretty close to a god." Indeed, Babe Ruth is one of baseball's legendary figures, a player unlike anyone before or since. His booming home runs changed the game forever. There will never, ever be another ballplayer like the Babe.

Baseball historians consider George Herman "Babe" Ruth one of the greatest players in the history of baseball, a star both on the mound and at the plate. During his first six seasons in the major leagues, Babe Ruth was one of the most successful pitchers in baseball, winning eighty-nine regular season games and three more for the Boston Red Sox in the World Series. Then he became the greatest slugger of his time, hitting home runs faster and farther than anyone who had ever played the game. He played the bulk of his career with the New York Yankees and ended with 714 home runs, a record that held until Hank Aaron broke it in 1974.

Yet for all his individual accomplishments, Babe Ruth was also a team player. He helped the Red Sox to three pennants and world championships. Then, after he was purchased by the Yankees after the 1919 season, Ruth led New York to seven pennants and four world championships, creating the Yankee dynasty that continues to this day.

But statistics and championships don't even begin to tell his story, for in addition to his accomplishments on the field, Ruth is unquestionably the most beloved baseball player in history. Baseball fans loved him for his talent, his generous personality, his ready smile, and his enormous heart. Ruth never lost sight of the fact that baseball was a game meant to be *played*. He was like an oversized kid, and he played baseball with simple joy.

Even today, nearly sixty years after his death in 1948, he remains the most popular baseball player of all time. Wherever kids gather to play baseball, young boys and girls still step up to the plate and dream of being Babe Ruth.

Yet few people realize what a difficult life Babe Ruth had, particularly when he was young. Due to his harsh upbringing, Ruth entered adulthood still thinking and acting like a child. He struggled most of his adult life to behave responsibly. For all his accomplishments on the field, Ruth's greatest victories were with himself.

Babe Ruth began life in Baltimore, Maryland, on February 6, 1895, as George Herman Ruth Jr., the firstborn child of two German Americans, George and Kate Ruth. From the start, the young family had a tough time. George Ruth Sr. had trouble finding work and had to leave Kate home alone with their son. But Kate was not a strong woman. Her illnesses prevented her from giving George Ruth Jr. as much attention as he needed. And when his sister, Mary Margaret, was born, five-year-old George was left to take care of himself as best he could.

Babe Ruth later admitted that he "was a bad kid," who "had no sense of right or wrong." Every morning he took to the streets with other unfortunate boys. Although they often played children's games, including baseball, without adult supervision, they frequently caused trouble. They stole food and money, committed vandalism, chewed tobacco, and fought among themselves and against children from other neighborhoods.

Young George rarely went to school. His parents tried to force him to go, but even beatings with a leather strap couldn't make him obey. Every day he became more uncontrollable. When he wasn't on the streets, he hung around the saloon his father owned — hardly a good place for a young boy to grow up. At an age when he should have been learning to read and write, he was drinking alcohol and stealing whiskey from customers.

One night, when George was seven years old, police were called to break up a brawl in the saloon. Afterward, a neighbor told the authorities that she had noticed George was in the saloon when he should have been attending school. The Ruths were ordered to send George to Saint Mary's Industrial School for Boys in the city of Baltimore.

Operated by the Xaverian Brothers of the Catholic

4

Church, St. Mary's was a training school for orphans, delinquents, and other poor young boys in need of help. More than eight hundred boys, ranging from the age of seven to eighteen, lived and studied at St. Mary's. Discipline under the brothers was strict. The boys were told what to do and when to do it. The students, who referred to themselves as "inmates," all slept in dormitories and were not allowed to leave St. Mary's without supervision.

Young George arrived at St. Mary's on June 13, 1902. Its imposing gray stone buildings and high wooden fence made it look like a prison. George didn't understand what St. Mary's was or why he was there. When his father escorted him to the school office, said good-bye, and left, George (the foul-mouthed, tobacco-chewing street urchin) suddenly discovered he wasn't so tough. Alone and afraid, he began to cry.

Fortunately, the Xaverians understood young boys like George. They knew such boys weren't bad — they just needed someone to pay attention to them and provide them with some direction, discipline, and love. They tried to provide each boy with an education and a skill that would eventually allow each of them to earn a living and become a good, responsible citizen.

George was kept so busy at St. Mary's that he didn't have time to get into trouble. All the boys awoke each morning at six, attended church, ate breakfast, and then spent five hours in school either learning academic subjects or studying for a trade. After a two-hour break for lunch and recess, they spent another two hours either in class or, if they were over twelve years old, working. Before dinner the boys were encouraged to play sports. They were then allowed to read for forty-five minutes before going to bed at 8:15. They attended school five days a week plus a half day on Saturday. After church services on Sundays they were free to participate in school sports, play in the band, and take part in other similar activities.

At first, George hated St. Mary's. No one had ever told him when to get up in the morning, when to eat, what to wear or do, or when to go to bed. After all, he had always done as he pleased before, and now suddenly the brothers were telling him what to do every minute of the day.

6

Each brother was assigned eight or ten boys to watch over. Brother Matthias, the head of discipline at St. Mary's, was assigned to look after young George Ruth. An enormous man who stood nearly six and a half feet tall and weighed nearly three hundred pounds, Matthias looked as if he could break a person in half with his bare hands.

But Brother Matthias didn't use force. He was firm, but gentle and patient. Although the boys called him "the boss," they weren't afraid of Brother Matthias. He treated each student with respect.

Brother Matthias took a special interest in young George, who could neither read nor write and had no idea how to behave properly. Ever so slowly, George began to respond to the attention. No adult had ever taken an interest in him. He began working hard at school and at his trade, shirtmaking, just to make Brother Matthias happy. A word or look of praise from Brother Matthias made George feel proud.

Brother Matthias loved baseball and was a good player himself. He wowed the students at St. Mary's by hitting long fly balls while holding the bat with only one hand.

George loved playing baseball, too. Nearly every afternoon, he played pickup games and practiced batting. On the weekends he played for several teams run by St. Mary's. These teams were made up of players of different ages from the various shop programs and dormitories. Some of the teams represented St. Mary's against other institutions. From Saturday afternoon through Sunday, George often played games with five or six different teams.

Everyone soon discovered that George was one of the best hitters at the school. He was big for his age, well coordinated, wiry, and strong. Although he played all positions, his strong arm often earned him a place behind the plate as a catcher. A lefty, he wasn't even bothered by the fact that he had to wear a left-handed catcher's mitt. Instead, he perfected a method of catching the ball, flipping it in the air, tucking the glove under his right arm, then snagging the ball with his throwing hand. Even with the extra time it took to do this maneuver, his arm was so powerful he could still throw out runners trying to steal.

Brother Matthias made sure that George didn't stray, even on the baseball diamond. One day, the pitcher for George's team was getting hit hard and George started laughing at him and making cruel comments. Brother Matthias listened for a while, then went up to George and said, "All right, George. *You* pitch."

George's jaw dropped. "I don't know how to pitch," he stammered.

"You must know a lot about pitching," Brother Matthias replied, "to know that your friend isn't any good. Go out there and show us how it is done."

George realized the brother was serious. He took the ball, walked to the mound, and stood there awkwardly as the other boys laughed at him.

But they didn't laugh for long. George may not have known a lot about pitching, but he did have a strong arm. He pitched well, and from then on took regular turns on the mound. But he had also learned an important lesson.

Periodically, George would return to live at home with his parents and sister. But without St. Mary's structure and discipline, he soon fell back into bad habits and his father would send him back to St. Mary's, where Brother Matthias always welcomed him back.

In 1908, when George was thirteen, he left St. Mary's again. This time, he managed to stay out of serious trouble for almost two years. Then his mother died. His father returned him to St. Mary's. This time, he was not scheduled to be released until he was twenty-one years old, and an adult.

Apart from a few scrapes with other boys, George rarely got into trouble at St. Mary's. While he wasn't much of a student, he had beautiful handwriting and was one of the best shirtmakers at the school. Years later, he would brag to his major league teammates that he could make a shirt in fifteen minutes, and they'd smile when they saw him carefully ironing his shirts. Sometimes George's teammates would even bring him their own laundry to iron!

The other boys at St. Mary's were always thrilled when he came back. With George Ruth on their team, St. Mary's was difficult to beat. Not only was he the best pitcher at the school, he was also the best hitter. In one season he hit more than sixty home runs!

Soon he was too good for the competition provided by St. Mary's opponents. Brother Matthias arranged for George to play ball on the weekends for local amateur and semipro teams made up of other teenagers and young adults. Stories about the young ballplayer named Ruth began to appear in Baltimore newspapers. By 1913 he was one of the best-known amateur players in the Baltimore area.

The best team in Baltimore was the professional Baltimore Orioles of the International League. Owner Jack Dunn, known as a shrewd judge of talent, scoured the area for ballplayers.

During the summer of 1913, former major league pitcher Joe Engel saw eighteen-year-old George pitch a game against Mount St. Mary's, a college team. George struck out eighteen of the first twenty men he faced. Engel immediately knew that George, who now stood six feet two inches tall and weighed 170 pounds, was something special.

The next day, Engel bumped into Dunn. He told him about the left-handed pitcher named Ruth and said, "He's got real stuff."

Dunn respected Engel's opinion. Several other youngsters from St. Mary's had done well in professional baseball. So in February of 1914, Dunn paid a visit to St. Mary's.

The Orioles were about to start spring training

and Dunn needed to stock his team with prospects. He met with Brother Paul, the school superintendent, and told him he was interested in signing the young left-handed pitcher with "stuff." Brother Paul wasn't surprised. For several months there had been rumors that Dunn was interested in George. With Brother Paul's permission, George worked out for Dunn. The club owner was impressed and wanted to sign him.

There was just one problem. George was only nineteen years old. St. Mary's was George's legal guardian and he was supposed to stay at the school until age twenty-one.

But Brother Paul was a baseball fan, too, and he knew that a chance to play professional baseball was a wonderful opportunity for George. He made arrangements to make Jack Dunn George's legal guardian.

Dunn offered George a contract of six hundred dollars for the season. When George heard that, he couldn't believe it. He had never imagined that it was possible to be *paid* to play baseball. George had never had more than a dollar or two in his pocket. Six hundred dollars seemed like all the money in the world. He eagerly agreed to become a professional baseball player.

George gathered up his few belongings in a cheap suitcase and walked out of St. Mary's, leaving with Dunn for spring training in Fayetteville, North Carolina. Then he paused outside the large iron gate and said good-bye to Brother Matthias, thanking him for all his help. George was excited but Matthias also saw that he was a little scared, just as he had been when he first arrived at St. Mary's years earlier. Matthias told him not to worry. "You'll make it, George," he said. Then George walked off with Dunn.

On February 27, 1914, the last entry under the name George Ruth in St. Mary's records reads simply, "He is going to join Balt. Baseball team."

★ CHAPTER TWO ★

1914

Dunn's Babe

When Ruth left St. Mary's, he knew little of the outside world. He had never been away from Baltimore before. He had never lived alone, bought his own clothes, or cooked his own meals. All he knew how to do was play baseball and make shirts.

On the train ride south, Ruth spent most of his time gazing out the window. When it was time to go to bed, one of the Oriole players had to explain to him how to fold down the sleeping berth. He also played a trick on the raw rookie.

In the berth was a small mesh clothes hammock. The veteran player told Ruth, "That's for your pitching arm." When Ruth went to bed, he dutifully placed his left arm in the hammock. When he awoke the next morning his arm was stiff and sore from hanging in a hammock all night. When the veterans saw him rubbing his arm, they all got a good laugh.

After the team checked into their hotel in Fayetteville, they went to the dining room for breakfast. George looked at the menu and wasn't quite sure what to do next. He didn't have much money and had never ordered from a menu.

Another veteran saw the puzzled look on his face and explained that the team paid for their meals during spring training. "Order anything you want," he told him.

Ruth couldn't believe it. He ordered pancakes and ham, wolfed them down, and then ordered another helping. He made quick work of the second order, and then asked for a third stack of pancakes and more ham. His teammates had long since finished eating and just stared at him in wonder. They had never seen anyone eat so much.

Everything was brand new to Ruth. He had never seen an elevator and was fascinated, spending hours riding up and down. He had never ridden a bicycle either. Every time he saw one he jumped on for a teetering ride. The other players couldn't help laughing at him. They had never seen anyone have so much fun.

Once he was out on the ball field, however, no one laughed. Ruth was impressive both on the mound and at the plate. In one scrimmage on March 7, Ruth walloped a home run into the cornfield beyond right field. Local fans recalled only one other ball hit so far, by former Olympian and major leaguer Jim Thorpe, when he had played minor league baseball in Fayetteville. But Ruth's blast traveled some sixty feet farther than Thorpe's. A headline in one Baltimore newspaper announced: "Ruth Makes Mighty Clout." In a few more seasons, such headlines would become familiar.

All spring Ruth was the big story for the Orioles. After only two weeks in camp Dunn told a newspaper, "Babe Ruth will definitely be staying with the team."

The story of how Ruth got the nickname is uncertain, but according to most accounts Ruth's Baltimore teammates dubbed him "Babe" because he was so young and inexperienced, like a baby. They would call him "Dunn's babe." Ruth wasn't bothered by the nickname, and although for a number of years the newspapers would still call him "George," everyone who knew him called him "Babe."

Dunn considered Babe Ruth a pitcher. Just three weeks after Ruth joined the Orioles, Dunn tapped him to pitch an exhibition game against the Philadelphia Athletics, the defending world champions of the major leagues.

Most rookie pitchers would have been nervous, but not Ruth. He barely followed major league baseball at St. Mary's and didn't even know the names of the players. Although the Athletics peppered him with thirteen hits, Ruth stayed cool and held them to only two runs, beating the champs 6–2!

The regular season began in late April. The Orioles returned to Baltimore and Ruth received his first paycheck of fifty dollars. He immediately went out and bought a motorcycle. Although Dunn was scared Ruth would crash and get hurt, he couldn't keep Ruth off the bike. The sight of Babe Ruth tearing around the city on the bike soon became familiar.

Ruth pitched his first regular season game on April 22 against Buffalo. After a shaky start, he settled down and spun a six-hit shutout. The Orioles won 6–0, with Babe knocking two singles.

Unfortunately, hardly anyone saw him. One year earlier, a new major league, the Federal League, had placed a team in Baltimore called the Terrapins. Local baseball fans all but ignored the Orioles. Dunn knew that unless the Orioles started drawing some fans he would soon go broke.

Dunn hoped Ruth, as a Baltimore native, would bring people back to the park. Although Babe didn't win every game he pitched, he was clearly one of the best rookies in the league. In fact, by mid-May, Dunn became concerned that the Terrapins would try to lure him away with a big salary. He tripled Ruth's pay to $1,800 for the season.

Keyed by the performances of Ruth and another rookie pitcher, Ernie Shore, in June, the Orioles won thirteen in a row. Yet Baltimore fans continued to ignore the Orioles — and Dunn was losing money fast. Even though the Federal League was also having financial trouble, Dunn was afraid he would run out of cash before the season was over. In early July, despite the fact that Baltimore was in first place, Dunn decided to sell players to raise some money. Within a few days, Ruth, pitcher Ernie Shore, and catcher Ben Egan's contracts were purchased by the Boston Red Sox for a total of $25,000.

The Red Sox were one of the most successful

franchises in baseball, world champions in both 1903 and 1912. But in 1914, the Red Sox were rebuilding for the future. Owner Joseph Lannin and manager Bill Carrigan hoped that Ruth and Shore would anchor the pitching staff.

Ruth left for Boston by train and arrived at Back Bay Station on July 11. In the past six months he had gone from being a student at St. Mary's Industrial School for Boys to a professional ball player with one of the strongest teams in the major leagues. But despite this huge change, Ruth himself stayed much the same.

As soon as he arrived in Boston, he checked into a hotel and then sought out a place to eat. He found Lander's Coffee Shop and ordered a big meal. As he ate he told his waitress, a pretty young woman named Helen Woodford, all about his trip to Boston. Ruth would return to Lander's many times in the next months and become very close to Helen. But on July 11, he couldn't stay long to chat. Fenway Park was calling.

✷ CHAPTER THREE ✷

1914–1918

Boston's Babe

The Red Sox were in sixth place with a record of 40–38 when Ruth joined the team. Manager Bill Carrigan was already looking ahead to next season and wanted to see how close his new players were to being able to help the club win. When Babe arrived at Fenway Park on July 11, 1914, Carrigan told him to start warming up because he was going to be on the mound that afternoon against the Cleveland Indians.

Some players might have been nervous, being put into play so soon. But not Ruth. Over the first six innings he held the Indians in check, giving up only six hits and one run before tiring in the seventh inning. The Red Sox and Ruth won the game, 4–3.

However, over the next month Carrigan rarely

used Ruth. Before Ruth became a regular on the mound, he needed to break some habits — such as the one he had of curling his tongue in the corner of his mouth when he was going to throw a curve ball, something he probably didn't realize he was doing, but hitters picked up on soon enough.

Carrigan was just as concerned with Ruth's adjustments to big league life. After living a sheltered life in St. Mary's, Ruth was making up for lost time. He stayed out all hours of the night, often letting "friends" take advantage of him and his newfound money.

His fellow ballplayers didn't quite know what to think of the newcomer. He was obviously a talented ballplayer, but he didn't behave like a rookie. Most young players are intimidated by older players, but not Ruth. He insisted on taking batting practice, something pitchers, particularly rookie pitchers, just didn't do. When the veterans complained, Ruth stood his ground. He argued with umpires, and on one occasion was even thrown out of a game. He didn't bother to learn anyone's name and called everyone "Kid," even players much older than he was. In the clubhouse he played practical jokes and tried to get other players to wrestle.

Off the field, Ruth was still learning how to act and behave. On the road he shared a hotel room with Ernie Shore. When Shore complained to Ruth that he was using Shore's toothbrush, Babe quipped, "That's all right. I don't mind." Shore just shook his head in wonder. Ruth could be aggravating, but it was hard to stay angry at him. He was just a big kid trying to catch up in a hurry.

In mid-August the Red Sox arranged to send Ruth to another club owned by Lannin, the Providence Grays of the International League. Ruth needed to pitch, not sit on the bench, and the Grays were fighting for the pennant.

Although Ruth was sad to leave Boston — and Helen — Providence was only forty miles south. Ruth gave the Grays a much-needed boost. He learned fast and over the remainder of the season won nine games out of ten.

On September 5, he did something else for the first time as a professional. While twirling a shutout, he also hit his first home run. The Grays went on to win the pennant.

After the victory, Ruth rejoined Boston for the last ten days of the season. He also rejoined Helen at Lander's. One day, while eating his usual enormous breakfast, Ruth turned to her and said while chewing, "Hey hon, how about you and me getting married?" It wasn't the most romantic proposal in history, but Helen said yes. They married in Baltimore soon after the season ended.

In March of 1915 Babe joined the team for spring training in Hot Springs, Arkansas. Ruth quickly developed a reputation as one of the most promising players in the game, and one of the most problematic.

By day, Ruth was securing a place as one of the team's best pitchers, and his batting performances during practice and exhibition games began to attract attention. At that time, the home run was a rarity. Players who hit ten or twelve for an entire season were considered power hitters. Most batters just tried to make contact and get base hits.

But not the Babe. He swung from his heels at every pitch and didn't seem worried when he missed the ball. In fact, fans enjoyed watching him swing and miss almost as much as they did watching him connect, for when Ruth missed a pitch he spun almost completely around. Yet when he did hit the ball, it was a wonder. The ball soared through the sky longer and farther than anyone had ever seen.

Off the field, however, Ruth was a terror. Hot Springs was a party town and Ruth stayed out all hours of the night. Carrigan tried to keep him in check with small fines and lectures, but Ruth usually paid him little attention. He was now twenty-one years old, an official adult. He enjoyed doing whatever he wanted, and he wanted to do everything all at once.

Ruth opened the season as one of Boston's top pitchers, but in his first four games he won only one. Then, on May 6, he turned his season — and perhaps his career — around, both on the mound and at the plate.

Carrigan picked him to start a game against the Yankees. After two scoreless innings, Ruth came to bat in the third against pitcher Jack Warhop.

At the time, the Yankees didn't have their own field. They played at the New York Giants' home ballpark, the cavernous Polo Grounds. Although the fences were relatively close right down the lines, elsewhere they were among the most distant in the game. At the Polo Grounds it was far more common to hit an inside-the-park home run rather than hitting one over the fence.

Ruth, however, always swung for the fences. Warhop delivered a pitch and Ruth swung as hard as he could. The ball hit the bat squarely and a loud *crack* echoed through the park. The drive soared high to right center field and just kept going, up and up, before finally landing in the upper deck of the right field grandstand. Ruth jogged around the bases with his first big league home run as the startled crowd buzzed with excitement. No one could recall ever seeing a ball hit that far in the Polo Grounds before. In a New York newspaper the next day, a reporter accurately referred to it as a "mighty homer."

Although the Red Sox lost the game 4–3 in thirteen innings, Ruth pitched the entire game and impressed his teammates with his batting and his solid pitching. The game gave manager Carrigan confidence in Ruth and, more importantly, gave Babe Ruth confidence in himself. For the remainder of the year he won another seventeen games and lost only once, finishing 18–6 while cracking two more home runs.

Boston's other pitchers were even better and with a batting attack led by future Hall of Fame outfielder Tris Speaker, the Red Sox won the pennant and the right to play the Philadelphia Phillies in the World Series. Ruth was thrilled and looked forward to pitching.

The Phillies featured a potent offense led by Gavvy Cravath, who had hit a record 24 home runs, many of them into the short porch in left field in the Phillies' home park, the Baker Bowl. Fans wondered if Boston's pitching could shut Cravath down.

So did Boston manager Bill Carrigan. Most right-handed batters hit left-handed pitching well and he didn't want a left-handed pitcher to face Cravath in Philadelphia. In the first two games he pitched two right-handers, Ernie Shore and Rube Foster. Apart from a pinch-hitting appearance, Ruth sat on the bench as the Sox split the first two games. As he recalled later, "I ate my heart out."

He confronted Carrigan, demanding to know why

he wasn't pitching. Carrigan didn't like Ruth's "me first" attitude, and when the series returned to Boston for game three, he passed over Ruth once more and pitched lefty Dutch Leonard. The Red Sox arranged to play their home games in more spacious Braves Field rather than Fenway Park, both to attract more fans and make it harder for Cravath to hit home runs. The veteran Leonard kept Cravath in the ballpark and won, putting Boston up in the Series. Then, in games four and five, Ernie Shore and Rube Foster pitched Boston to victory and the Red Sox won the world championship.

In the midst of the team celebration, Ruth was heartbroken. Even though he earned more than $3,600 as a member of the winning team, he was disappointed that he didn't get to pitch.

That winter Ruth and his wife again returned to Baltimore. When he returned for spring training, his teammates and manager hardly recognized him. Ruth had gained twenty pounds during the off-season, making him much stronger. He was clearly becoming a better pitcher, and his fastball was now one of the best in baseball.

However, Boston owner Joseph Lannin was having financial trouble. Over the past few seasons he had paid big salaries to keep players from jumping to the Federal League. The league collapsed in the off-season, and now Lannin wanted to save some money. He sold star outfielder Tris Speaker to Cleveland.

The 1916 Red Sox would have to win or lose with their pitching. Fortunately, Babe Ruth emerged as one of the best pitchers in the league, and at times gave notice that he was one of the most dangerous hitters, too.

On his way to a record of 23–12 with a league best earned run average of 1.75, Ruth beat Washington Senators pitcher Walter Johnson, arguably the greatest pitcher in baseball, four different times, all by the score of 1–0. He also hit .272 with three home runs, tied for best on the team.

Paced by Ruth's performance, the Red Sox fought off several challengers and won the American League pennant for the second consecutive season. They played the Brooklyn Dodgers in the World Series.

After Ernie Shore pitched and won game one, Carrigan selected Babe Ruth to pitch the second game of the World Series. Ruth was thrilled with the assignment and determined to win. In the first inning, however, he got off to a bad start. Brooklyn outfielder Hy Myers hit a line drive to center field. It skipped past the Boston centerfielder and rolled to the wall. Myers raced around the bases for a home run. However, Ruth bounced back and in the third inning he knocked in the tying run with a ground ball.

Inning after inning, the score stayed knotted at 1–1 as Brooklyn pitcher Sherry Smith equaled Ruth's effort. The game entered extra innings as the sun slowly set.

Finally, in the fourteenth inning Boston pushed across a run to win the game, 2–1. After the first inning run, Ruth had pitched thirteen innings of shutout ball, one of the best performances in World Series history. After the game he gave Bill Carrigan a huge hug and bellowed, "I told you I could take care of those National Leaguers!" Boston went on to win the series in five games to become world champions for the second time.

In the off season, Lannin sold the Red Sox to Harry Frazee, an extremely successful producer of

Broadway plays. Manager Bill Carrigan retired and was replaced by Jack Barry.

The year 1917 brought other changes, too. The United States declared war on Germany and became involved in World War I. The government instituted a draft to build up the military. Baseball, like all parts of American life, was thrown into turmoil.

Ruth himself was also going through some personal turmoil. On the field, he pitched just as well as he had in 1916. But off the field he began to spin out of control. He was famous now, and rich, earning more than $5,000 a season. He still liked to party, and he didn't respect manager Barry as much as he did Bill Carrigan. Ruth started drinking more and staying out all hours of the night.

His on-field behavior started to get out of control as well. On June 23, in a game against the Senators, he became enraged when umpire Brick Owens called his first four pitches balls. As the leadoff hitter jogged to first base on a walk, Ruth rushed the plate and confronted Owen. When the umpire told Ruth he would throw him from the game if he didn't settle down, Ruth screamed, "Throw me out and I'll punch you in the jaw!"

Owen tossed Ruth from the game — and Ruth threw a punch, striking Owen on the side of his head and knocking him to the ground. Babe received a well deserved one-week suspension and was fined $100. Fortunately for the Red Sox, Ernie Shore came on in relief and didn't give up a hit the rest of game.

That season, Ruth won 24 games, but it was the White Sox who won the pennant, besting Boston by nine games. When the season was over, Babe and Helen didn't return to Baltimore as before, but stayed near Boston on a farm he purchased and named "Home Plate." Although he enjoyed being on the farm with Helen, the bright lights of Boston proved too attractive to the fun-loving ballplayer. Ruth spent much of his time carousing in the city. He loved driving — especially driving fast. Once that off-season he narrowly avoided being killed when he crashed his car into a trolley.

Still, when spring training started in 1918, Ruth was there and ready to play his best. Because of the draft and the war, the Red Sox, like many clubs, didn't have quite enough players. Even manager Jack Barry had joined the military and was replaced by Ed Barrow. As a result, Babe Ruth, the pitcher, turned into Babe Ruth, the slugger, outfielder, and first baseman. He hit several long home runs and fans started turning out as much to see him hit as they did to see him pitch.

But when the season officially opened, Ruth returned to full-time mound duty. In a 5–4 loss to the Yankees on May 4, he slugged a long home run into the upper deck of the Polo Grounds. In the next game, he played first base — and hit another long home run. Then he then did it again in his next contest, this time off the great Walter Johnson. By May 11 he was leading the league in hitting. Over the next few months he was the sensation of baseball, hitting four more home runs.

Ruth enjoyed pitching, but he *loved* hitting. Nothing in his life gave him as big a thrill as smashing a long fly ball for a home run and then jogging around the bases while the fans roared.

And the fans did roar for him. Ruth was already one of the most popular players in the game. Kids loved him and Ruth, nothing but a big kid himself, loved being around kids. On occasion he was spotted after games roughhousing with kids in local city parks.

By mid-summer Ruth had hit a league best of eleven home runs and decided he didn't want to pitch anymore. But the Red Sox had enough hitting; they needed him on the mound.

Ruth refused, and in mid-summer he left the team and joined a semi-pro club in Maryland that offered him a big salary. The Red Sox threatened to file suit to prevent Ruth from playing for another team. His Boston teammates were also upset. They liked Ruth but thought he was selfish for abandoning them in mid-season. After realizing the Red Sox could take him to court for breaking his contract, Ruth reluctantly returned to the team and took his regular turn in the rotation, making only an occasional appearance on the field as his batting average slumped.

Ruth came back just in time to save the season. He won nine of his last eleven starts and the Red Sox took command of the American League and won the pennant. Ruth finished the season with a record of 13–7 and a .300 batting average. The Red

Sox then faced the Chicago Cubs in the World Series.

The Red Sox started Ruth in game one in Chicago. He was magnificent and shut out the Cubs. George Whiteman, the Red Sox left fielder, was the other big hero of the game, cracking two hits to help Boston score the only run they needed in the 1–0 victory.

The two teams split the next two games and then traveled by train to Boston. On the journey back home, Ruth started goofing around — running through the train, grabbing straw hats and punching holes in them. Then, just before the train reached Boston, he ran out of straw hats to destroy. Still bubbling with energy, he scuffled with teammate Walt Kinney. He took a swing at Kinney — and accidentally punched his left hand into the steel wall of the train car.

Ruth howled in pain. The middle knuckle of his pitching hand started to swell. Manager Barry was understandably upset. "You fool," he snarled. "You're supposed to pitch tomorrow!"

A chagrined Ruth knew he'd messed up. He gritted his teeth and said, "I'll be okay. I'll pitch tomorrow."

Sure enough, Ruth took the mound for the fourth

game of the series. His swollen hand made it difficult for him to grip the ball. Despite giving up a large number of hits and walks, he managed to keep the Cubs in check.

In the fourth inning he came to bat with two men on base. After working the count to 3–2, he smacked a long drive over the head of the right fielder for a triple. As one newspaper reporter put it, the hit made "a sound like rifle shot [that] echoed through the park." Boston led 2–0 at that point.

Unfortunately, Ruth tired in the eighth inning and the Cubs scored twice to tie the game. Few people realized it at the time, but these two runs ended an unbelievable streak. Ruth had pitched $29^2/_3$ consecutive scoreless innings in the World Series, a new record that would stand for another 42 years until broken by Yankee pitcher Whitey Ford.

In the Boston eighth, the Red Sox managed to push across another run to go ahead 3–2. Ruth started the ninth, and then he left for a reliever. The Red Sox won to go ahead in the series, three games to one.

Two days later, the Red Sox took the world championship. Ruth received credit for two wins, but apart from a late appearance in the outfield in the final game, he sat on the bench the rest of the series.

It had been an incredible year for the Babe, and one that was never to be repeated. No one knew it yet, but Ruth's career as a pitcher — and as a member of the Boston Red Sox — was just about over.

★ CHAPTER FOUR ★

1919–1923

Becoming the Bambino

On November 11, 1918, World War I ended and baseball returned to normal. Most of the players the Red Sox had lost during the war rejoined the team. The defending champions looked even stronger than before.

Buoyed by his stellar season the previous year, Ruth felt he deserved more money. The trouble was, he already had a contract for $7,000 a year. When Harry Frazee refused to raise his salary, Ruth held out, refusing to play in 1919 unless he received a big raise. Spring training had already started when Frazee reluctantly signed him to a new three-year contract worth $10,000 a season, one of the biggest contracts in baseball. Ruth reported to camp in Tampa, Florida, and immediately got everyone's attention.

In the off-season Ruth had come to a decision. Even though he was one of the best hurlers in baseball, he didn't want to pitch anymore. He just wanted to hit. So the first time he took the field, in the first exhibition game against the New York Giants, he played the outfield.

He came to bat in the second inning. The pitcher threw and Ruth took a great wallop. *Boom!* The bat connected with the ball and made an unmistakable sound. In a heartbeat the ball sailed over the right-fielder's head and just kept going. By the time the outfielder hopped over the short fence and retrieved the ball, Ruth had long since reached home plate.

After the game several people attempted to measure how far the home run had traveled. According to some accounts the ball traveled an amazing 600 feet!

When the Red Sox opened the season a few weeks later, Ruth was still in the outfield. In less than a week, he found himself in big trouble.

While the Red Sox played in Washington, Ruth stayed out all night. A hotel worker woke Barrow when Ruth returned at six in the morning. The manager knocked on Ruth's door. Ruth, still dressed and smoking a pipe, quickly jumped under the covers,

Before he was a Boston Red Sox pitcher and a New York Yankees slugger, Babe Ruth played for Baltimore in the International League in 1914. This is his baseball card for that year.

An undated photo shows pitcher Babe Ruth in his Red Sox uniform. His ability to slug home runs had not yet been discovered by the ball club.

Home run! Yankee Babe Ruth, the Sultan of Swat, clouts one into the stands in this undated photo.

Babe Ruth makes baseball history when he slugs in his sixtieth home run on September 30, 1927.

A rare shot of the Babe sliding into home plate. Usually he arrived standing up!

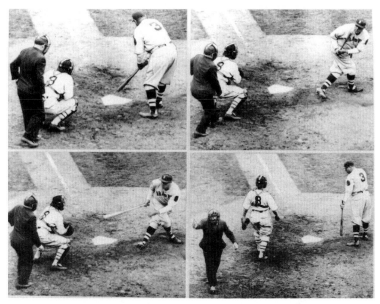

Even Babe Ruth's strikes were powerful! In upper left corner, he taps the plate. In upper right, he swings and misses for strike one. Strike two follows, then strike three and he's out.

—

Babe Ruth embraces an emotional Lou Gehrig on July 4, 1939—the day Gehrig called himself "the luckiest man in the world."

Fans always flocked to Babe for autographs. In 1947, he signed a ball for a young female ballplayer.

pulled them up to his neck, and told the manager to come in.

Barrow entered, walked over to the bed, and pulled the covers down, revealing Ruth still in his street clothes. He gave Ruth a disgusted look and snapped, "I'll see you at the ballpark!" Later, he suspended Ruth for a day and gave him a piece of advice. "Turn your life around," Barrow told him.

For a while, Ruth heeded the advice, at least off the field. On the field, however, he struggled. Once the season started his big bat was silent and the move to the outfield seemed like a big mistake. By the first of June he was one of the worst hitters in the league. The Red Sox weren't scoring runs with Ruth in the lineup and they missed him on the pitching mound. The World Series champs were already out of the pennant race, their season effectively over.

Barrow and Frazee begged Ruth to return to the mound. He reluctantly agreed, but only if he was still allowed to play the outfield between starts. Almost immediately his bat perked up and he started hitting home runs at a record rate. It was too late to help the Sox that season, but fans began to turn out in droves to see him hit, particularly in New York, where for some reason he always hit the ball better than anywhere else.

Ruth loved the attention and stayed hot for the rest of the season, breaking Cravath's record with twenty-nine home runs. He helped out on the mound occasionally, too, but the turnaround came too late for the Red Sox. They finished in sixth place.

Then Ruth made another bad mistake. Just a few days before the end of the season, he left without permission to play an exhibition game for extra money. That angered his teammates, manager Barrow, and Harry Frazee.

Over the past few seasons Frazee had been fighting with Ban Johnson, the President of the American League. Johnson didn't want Frazee to own the Red Sox anymore and Frazee didn't think Johnson should be league president. The other teams took sides, with the Red Sox, Yankees, and White Sox battling Johnson in the courts over a variety of issues.

In the midst of all this trouble, Frazee didn't need more aggravation from his players. Over the past few seasons Ruth had put himself above the team, running around all hours of the night and not taking care of himself. He was a great player, but he was also becoming a huge headache. When Ruth demanded yet another raise and a new contract, Frazee decided he'd had enough. He knew Ruth was a popular and talented player that many clubs would be interested in acquiring. He decided to sell Ruth while the price was high and rebuild.

The New York Yankees needed a star attraction. Since joining the American League in 1903, they had never won a pennant. But in 1919, new owners Jacob Ruppert and Cap Huston had money to spend. They decided to build the team around Babe Ruth, as a hitter, not a pitcher.

Harry Frazee held out until Ruppert and Huston offered him $100,000 for Ruth. Just before the New Year, Frazee agreed to sell Ruth to the Yankees.

Some fans and sportswriters in Boston were angry about the sale, believing that Frazee had thrown away their best player. Others agreed with Frazee who said "the Yankees are taking quite a risk" with Ruth. In New York, some thought Ruth would become a star and lead the Yankees to a pennant. Others worried that Ruth was too out of control and that he might never again hit as well as he had in 1919. The sale was a gamble on both sides.

Ruth played to the press in both places, telling Boston reporters he hated to leave and telling those in New York he was thrilled to be a Yankee. That thrill was made even sweeter when the Yankees gave him a new contract worth $20,000 a year in 1921 and 1922.

The Yankees got Ruth at a time when baseball was going through some changes. In August of 1919, a player named Ray Chapman was struck in the head by a pitch and died in a hospital twelve hours later. After Chapman's untimely death, Major League Baseball instigated some new rules about pitching. Spitballs were made illegal, for one thing. For another, new baseballs had to be used whenever the one in play became discolored. New balls were harder, brighter, easier to see, and also easier to hit for home runs than worn-out balls. For home run hitters like Ruth, new balls were good news.

The Yankees' home park, the Polo Grounds, was also tailor-made for a pull hitter like Ruth. The right-field fence was much closer than the one in Fenway Park. Although Ruth would have undoubtedly hit plenty of home runs if he had stayed in Boston, he never would have set the records he set at the Polo Grounds.

Baseball was also beginning to feel the effects of the recent "Black Sox" scandal. Rumors were swirling that in 1919 the Chicago White Sox had thrown the World Series. Although it would take nearly a year before the scope of the plot was fully known, baseball was in desperate need of a hero. Babe Ruth was ready-made for the role.

It didn't seem that way at first, however. Ruth got off to a rocky start with the Yankees. Although he hit well in the spring, his behavior raised many eyebrows. In the middle of one exhibition game, he went into the stands and tried to attack a fan who had been teasing him. He caused problems for management, too, when he insisted on playing center field. When manager Miller Huggins resisted, Ruth went over his head to make his case with the Yankee owners. They agreed, although eventually Ruth settled into right field.

Then the season began and all eyes turned to the newest Yankee. Unfortunately, on opening day Ruth misplayed a fly ball that cost his team a win. In his second game he struck out three times! Then the Yankees played the Red Sox in Boston. Ruth did nothing and the Red Sox swept New York. So far, the Babe was a big bust.

Things didn't improve when the Yankees played their first home game. Ruth swung too hard at a pitch in batting practice and separated his ribs. After that, swinging a bat was painful for him and he struck out repeatedly. By May 1, the Yankees were only 4–7. Meanwhile, the Red Sox were in first place — without Ruth.

Ruth's ribs finally healed by the beginning of May, and he finally hit his first home run as a Yankee, a long blast at the Polo Grounds. That belt seemed to shake him loose. For the rest of the season he blasted home run after home run and in mid-season New York surged into first place. On July 15, Ruth broke his own home run record when he smacked his thirtieth round-tripper of the season. Every home run he hit for the remainder of the season set a new record.

Baseball fans everywhere were thrilled, packing stadiums wherever the Yankees played. They may not all have been Yankee fans, but they were all Ruth fans.

There was something about Ruth that fans found irresistible. He did everything in a big way. Even his strikeouts were exciting, as the momentum of his swing nearly knocked him to the ground every time he missed. Ruth knew how to play to the crowd, and fans were thrilled when he tipped his cap and revealed his smiling, moon-shaped face after hitting a home run, or grimaced after missing a pitch, or bellowed a complaint to an umpire.

Around that time, George Herman "Babe" Ruth got a new nickname. Many of the fans living around Yankee Stadium were Italian. They christened Ruth "Bambino," which is Italian for "baby" or "babe." New York sportswriters also used nicknames when describing him, such as the "Colossus of Clout," the "Mauling Monarch," the "Prince of Pounders," and the "Sultan of Swat." They wrote about him every day throughout the season. Every home run he hit was news, and so was every strikeout.

However, despite Ruth's prodigious hitting, 1920 simply wasn't the Yankees' year. In August, Yankees pitcher Carl Mays accidentally hit Cleveland Indians shortstop Ray Chapman in the head with a pitch. Chapman died, and after the tragedy the Indians bounced back to take the pennant.

Ruth finished the season with a batting average of .376 with a record fifty-four home runs, a total that was higher than that hit by all but two teams in baseball. There seemed to be no limit to what he could accomplish. Fans wondered if he would one day hit sixty or even seventy home runs in a season.

His performance changed the game forever. After seeing what Ruth could accomplish, other players changed their approach at the plate. Instead of just trying to make contact, more hitters began to swing from their heels like Babe Ruth. Before Ruth, most batters hit home runs by accident. Now they tried to imitate Ruth. In a few years the home run would become more common.

Ruth soon cashed in on his fame. He starred in a movie called *Headin' Home,* endorsed all sorts of products, and had a sports column written under his name by sportswriter Christy Walsh. He also went on a long "barnstorming" trip, playing a series of exhibition games after the season and hitting home runs against local teams before thousands of fans. Although organized baseball considered such tours illegal, Ruth didn't care. He was the most famous man in America, and he was making more money off the field than on it.

Of course, having lots of cash made it even more difficult for Ruth to stay out of trouble. Even though a new law known as Prohibition, which banned the sale of alcohol, went into effect, that didn't slow down Ruth, who spent much of his time in what were known as "speakeasies," illegal taverns that served alcohol. Life in the off season was one big party, and he turned up for spring training covered in a thick layer of fat.

Ruth managed to get in shape in the spring and rapidly resumed his record hitting in 1921. Pitchers were afraid of him and rarely gave him a pitch to hit. When they did, he knocked it out of the park.

Ruth and the Yankees took the American League by storm. At the end of the season Ruth had increased his home run record to an incredible fifty-nine, and the Yankees won the pennant and the right to play the New York Giants in the World Series.

The Giants, led by feisty manager John McGraw,

were a terrific team. Unlike the Yankees, who waited for Ruth to hit home runs, the Giants still played baseball the old-fashioned way, scratching and clawing for runs with bunts, base hits, and stolen bases. McGraw, considered the best manager in baseball, promised everyone that his pitchers would shut down Ruth and the Yankees — a promise he made good on.

In a sense, the Yankees lost the series in the second game. After winning game one, the Yankees also took game two. But in the middle of the game, Ruth, who had already walked three times, slid roughly into third base. As he twisted away from the tag, he scraped his elbow.

Ruth shrugged off the injury, but in game three, a 13–5 Giant win, he scraped it again. By game four the elbow was infected and badly swollen. By the next game, he could barely see the bat, and struck out three times, collecting his only hit on a bunt. By then it was obvious he couldn't continue to play because of the pain. For the rest of the series he made only one appearance, as a pinch hitter.

Without Ruth, the Yankees were an average team.

The Giants stormed back to win the best-of-nine series five games to three. Despite his record 59 regular season home runs, 1921 ended in disappointment for Ruth.

After the season, baseball commissioner Kenesaw Mountain Landis warned Ruth not to go on another barnstorming tour. Ruth ignored him and went anyway. He felt as if he were bigger than the game.

He wasn't. In December Landis suspended him for the first six weeks of the 1922 season.

Fortunately, the Yankees had earned so much money the previous season that they were able to acquire a number of other valuable players, many from the Red Sox. Although they missed Ruth at the start of the season and sometimes struggled after his return, the Yankees still had enough firepower and pitching to win the pennant.

However, Ruth was in a slump, at least for him. His batting average dropped to .315 and he hit "only" thirty-five home runs, not enough to beat the new league leader, Ken Williams (of the St. Louis Browns), who hit thirty-nine.

Meanwhile, his behavior was once again a cause

for concern. When he returned to the team after the suspension, he was out of shape and never really got going. As the season progressed, he spent night after night out on the town and often showed up at the ballpark bleary-eyed. One of his Yankee roommates later said he didn't really room with Ruth, he roomed "with his suitcase," because Ruth was always out. On the field, Ruth argued with umpires and was suspended several times for using bad language. Manager Huggins was powerless to change him. Everybody was.

The Yankees met the Giants in the World Series for the second season in a row. This time, it wasn't even close. The Giants won in five games and Ruth was terrible, collecting only two hits.

At a banquet Ruth attended shortly after the end of the series, speaker after speaker lectured him about his behavior and the way in which he had disappointed not only his teammates but the fans. New York Mayor Jimmy Walker said, "You have let down the kids of America . . . they have seen their idol shattered and their dream broken." Babe Ruth was humiliated and told everyone, "I'm going back to my farm to get in shape."

His career was at a crossroads and he knew it. If he didn't do something fast, he wouldn't be Babe Ruth anymore. This time, he didn't have anyone like Brother Matthias to bail him out. Ruth would have to help himself. It was time for him to grow up, at least a little.

★ CHAPTER FIVE ★

1923–1925

Ups and Downs

Babe Ruth kept his promise that winter. He returned to his Massachusetts farm, reuniting with Helen after a long separation, and rarely ventured into the city. He stopped drinking, watched what he ate, and spent the winter doing farm work, skating, chopping wood, and going for long hikes. He knew he had messed up in 1922 and was determined to prove that he was still the best player in the game.

New York fans were looking forward to the 1923 season. At the cost of $2.5 million dollars, the Yankees had finally built their own ballpark, Yankee Stadium. The new park in the Bronx was huge, capable of holding more than 70,000 fans, most of whom were looking forward to seeing the Babe hit some home runs. The park designers had done what they could to satisfy them by making sure the fence in right field was short enough for Ruth to hit home runs with the same frequency he had at the Polo Grounds.

This year, the Bambino didn't let them down. He showed up at spring training in tremendous shape, weighing 209 pounds. And on opening day at Yankee Stadium he announced his return in dramatic fashion.

With the score 1–0 in favor of the Yankees in the fourth inning, Ruth came to bat. Boston pitcher Howard Ehmke let a ball over the plate and Ruth gave it everything he had.

The ball soared deep and high to right field as everyone in the stadium stood and craned their necks to watch the flight of the ball. When it finally came down it was ten rows deep in the right-field stands. Babe Ruth had hit the first home run in Yankee Stadium! After the Yankee victory that day, a sportswriter referred to the stadium as "the House that Ruth Built," a nickname that has stayed with it ever since.

For the rest of the season there was no stopping New York. Although Ruth didn't hit home runs quite as frequently as before, ending the season with only forty-one, he hit better than ever, staying above .400 for most of the year before finishing at .393. The Yankees won the pennant by sixteen games over Detroit. Once again, they played the New York Giants in the World Series.

Thus far, Ruth had done everything in New York but help the Yankees win a championship. For all his accomplishments he knew he wouldn't really be considered a success until the Yankees won the series. Giants' manager John McGraw entered the series confident. After all, his pitchers had shut down Ruth in both 1921 and 1922 by throwing him outside curve balls. "The same system," he said, "will suffice."

This time, however, Ruth was ready. He tripled in the first game, a Yankee loss, but in game two he broke loose with two long home runs and narrowly missed a third. Although the Giants won game three 1–0, the Giants chose to walk Ruth twice rather than let him hit. Then, in game four, Ruth and the Yankees took command and won the next two games to finally take the series away from their crosstown rivals.

Yankee owner Jake Ruppert was ecstatic. "Now I

have the greatest ballpark and the greatest team," he said. Everyone already knew he had the greatest player — Babe Ruth.

The following year, the cocky Yankees figured they'd win another world championship in 1924 just by showing up. Although Ruth had started drifting back to his old ways and was again gaining weight, most observers figured that the Yankees still had more than enough firepower and pitching to win.

But the overconfident Yankees got off to a slow start. Before the season they foolishly released pitcher Carl Mays. He later won twenty games for Cincinnati while the Yankee pitching staff fell apart. By mid-season the Yankees were battling Washington and Detroit for the pennant.

Ruth, however, was having another great year, just a shade below his performance in 1923. Still, despite cracking 46 home runs and hitting .378, he couldn't put the Yankees over the top. They finished second.

Unlike the previous winter, this year Ruth didn't take care of himself. Instead of spending the off-season on his farm, getting ready for the upcoming season, he ran all over the country eating, drinking, and partying way too much. By the time he started thinking about the upcoming season, he weighed nearly 260 pounds! He tried to lose weight, but he wasn't disciplined enough to turn down big meals, exercise regularly, and go to bed early. When spring training began, he was still overweight, drinking heavily, and staying up all hours of the night.

Manager Miller Huggins repeatedly cautioned Ruth about his behavior, but Ruth just laughed at him. Huggins was a little man and Ruth didn't take him seriously. Besides, despite being out of shape he hit nearly .500 in the spring. He felt indestructible.

Then, near the end of spring training, all the late nights, drinking binges, smoking, and overeating caught up with him. The Yankees were on their way back to New York when Ruth, who had been complaining of stomach cramps, collapsed on a train platform in North Carolina.

Rumors swept the country that he had died, but after a few days he felt a little better and left with Yankee scout Paul Krichell to rejoin the team. He made it as far as Washington, D.C., before collapsing again. This time he fell unconscious.

Krichell somehow got him on the train to New York. When the train pulled into the station, Ruth had to be removed through a window on a stretcher — he couldn't walk and was so fat that the stretcher could not be maneuvered down the aisle. He was rushed to St. Vincent's Hospital and admitted on April 9. He remained in the hospital for the next six weeks.

Over time, the illness became known as the "bellyache heard around the world," and it was often blamed on too many hot dogs and too much soda pop. But that wasn't the cause. Ruth was seriously ill. Although the exact nature of the illness remains a mystery, he did undergo a minor operation to remove an intestinal abscess. Some have speculated that he had some kind of embarrassing disease, while others believe Ruth may have been receiving treatment for alcoholism. Whatever the cause, he was very, very sick for a long time.

When he finally left the hospital on May 26, he didn't look like Babe Ruth. He had lost thirty pounds, and his legs were rail thin and shaky from lack of exercise. His gaunt face made him look twenty years older. Even when he felt well enough to play again, he didn't play like Babe Ruth.

The Yankees had struggled without him and were

already out of the race. Through June and July, Ruth hit only .250 with a handful of home runs. The only bright spot on the team was rookie first baseman Lou Gehrig, who was hitting nearly .300.

New York sportswriters looked at Ruth and saw a player near the end of his career. He was a thirty-year-old man who looked like he was fifty. Despite his weight loss in the hospital, he was still too heavy and waddled around the bases. A hard run left him weak. Pitchers weren't afraid of him anymore. On one occasion Huggins even removed Ruth from a game for a pinch hitter.

Incredibly, within weeks of leaving the hospital he resumed his late-night lifestyle. That didn't help his recovery. He had met another woman, Claire Hodgson, and wanted to marry her, but because he was Catholic he couldn't divorce Helen. On and off the field, Ruth was a mess.

It all came to a head on August 29 in St. Louis. Ruth stayed out past team curfew and got caught. When he arrived at the park the next day, Miller Huggins told him, "Don't bother getting dressed. I'm suspending you and fining you $5,000. You're to go back to New York."

"What?" Ruth bellowed. He couldn't believe Huggins would do that, but the manager had already checked with Jake Ruppert and the owner told him to do what he felt was best for the team. Ruth threatened his manager, saying, "If you were half my size I'd punch you."

Huggins stood his ground and didn't flinch. "If I were half your size, I'd punch *you*," he said. Then he told Ruth not to return to the ball club until he was ready to apologize, not only to Huggins but to his teammates.

Ruth was angry and hurt. He railed against Huggins to the press and said he was going to appeal to Commissioner Landis or to Jake Ruppert. He didn't think anyone could tell him what to do. After all, he was Babe Ruth. He foolishly believed that because he was so popular and famous either Landis or Ruppert would order Huggins to put him back in the lineup. Ruth told the press he expected Landis to "do the right thing," and that Huggins "has Ruppert buffaloed. Huggins is trying to make me the goat." Ruth wanted Huggins fired and said he would never play for him again. If the suspension was upheld, Ruth said he was prepared to quit the game.

But Ruth misread both Landis and Ruppert. Landis didn't even want to meet with him and announced that he supported the suspension. Ruppert was even more direct, saying, "I understand Ruth says he will not play for the Yankees as long as Huggins is manager. Well, Huggins will be manager as long as he wants to be." Ruth was shocked.

Everyone liked Ruth. Everyone wanted to see him play. But everyone agreed that unless he started taking care of himself and changed his ways, baseball and the Yankees were better off without him. No one was bigger than the game.

After a few days Ruth asked Huggins if he could apologize and the manager turned him down — he wanted Ruth to realize how serious the situation was. As Ruth waited on the sideline, he began to realize how much he enjoyed playing and how he was wasting his life. He even called Brother Matthias and spent several hours discussing his future.

Finally, after nine long days, Huggins agreed to meet Ruth. Babe approached his manager like an ashamed little boy and apologized profusely. Then Huggins told him he would have to make the same apology to his teammates.

The Yankees gathered in the clubhouse and Ruth sheepishly entered the room, nearly in tears. "I was wrong," he admitted. "I'm too hotheaded." He knew he had let everyone down. More importantly, he had let himself down, wasting his talent and ruining the season for his team and the fans.

Ruth was allowed to rejoin the team, but the season could not be saved. The Yankees finished seventh and Ruth hit only .290 with 25 home runs. Although Babe had always enjoyed the backing of the press, even the sportswriters had turned against him. Many believed he should retire and that the Yankees would be better off without him.

So far, despite hitting a record number of home runs, Ruth had yet to fulfill his promise as a Yankee. While they had won three pennants, they had won only one world championship and in the seasons after that Ruth had done little to excite New York's management, his teammates, or fans. Unless he permanently turned his life around soon, his career as a Yankee would be a failure.

✳ CHAPTER SIX ✳

1926–1928

The Greatest

The suspension finally shocked Ruth into taking his life and his career seriously. He separated from Helen, and she moved from the farm back to Boston. He felt badly about his marriage falling apart, but he knew he had hardly been the ideal husband. All winter long Ruth tried to make amends for his horrible performance in 1925.

He turned down a chance to make money on another exhibition tour. He wrote a magazine article in which he apologized to the fans and admitted he had acted like "a boob." Determined to get back in shape, he put himself in the hands of gym owner Artie McGovern.

It helped that he had the love and support of Claire Hodgson. Like Brother Matthias, Ruth respected her opinion. When she told him that he had to change, Ruth listened. He realized that if he did not, he would lose more than his baseball career. He might also lose her.

Every day he spent four hours at the gym, working out. At first the exercise sessions, which included long walks, handball, weightlifting, and steam baths, left him exhausted. But ever so slowly he began to lose weight and replace flab with muscle.

By February of 1926 he was ready to play again. He had lost nearly thirty pounds and almost ten inches from his waist. Although no one would ever accuse Ruth of being slender, he was once again a powerful athlete.

Meanwhile, the Yankees were invigorated by the addition of infielder Tony Lazzeri, a terrific hitter, and the continued improvement of first baseman Lou Gehrig, who was beginning to show that he was almost as dangerous at the plate as Ruth. Hodgson stayed close to Ruth all year and she kept him from running around all hours of the night.

The Yankees got off to a great start and just kept going. Babe Ruth wasn't just back, he was all the way back, hitting .372 and cracking 47 home runs while driving in 155. Tony Lazzeri and Lou Gehrig each knocked in over 100 runs as well, and the Yankees cruised to the pennant. They then met the St. Louis Cardinals in the World Series.

The Yankees were big favorites, but the Cardinals were a talented team. After New York won the first game, the Cardinals came back to win the next two. Ruth, in a post-season slump, collected only two singles in the first three games. Game four in St. Louis was a must-win for New York.

Ruth came to the plate determined to do what it took to give his team that win. In the first inning he hit the first pitch he saw for a home run. In the third inning he hit another home run. Then, in the sixth inning, he truly outdid himself.

With the count at three-and-two, Ruth swung and hit the ball as hard as possible. It soared deep to center field. Announcer Graham MacNamee was broadcasting the game to the nation over the radio, one of the first national broadcasts. Fans all over the country heard his description:

The Babe hits it into the centerfield bleachers for a home run! A home run! Did you hear what I said? Oh, what a shot! . . . This is a World

Series record, three home runs in one series game . . . They tell me that's the first ball ever hit into the center field stand. That's a mile and a half from here!

It wasn't quite that far, but it was the farthest ball ever hit in St. Louis. Even Cardinal fans applauded his hit, which was in fact the first ball ever hit into the centerfield bleachers. Not that the ball stopped there — it bounced out of the bleachers into the street!

No one knew, however, that the home run meant even more to a little boy listening to MacNamee's broadcast. Young Johnny Sylvester had been badly hurt in a fall from a horse and was laid up in a New York hospital. His father had asked for the Cardinals and Yankees to send him some autographed baseballs to cheer his son up. The teams did, and Ruth added a promise that he would hit a home run for Johnny. The boy heard MacNamee announce all three of Ruth's three home runs. The smile that lit his face didn't go away for days.

The Yankees won 10–5. They took the next game, too, thanks to a great save made by Ruth. The Yankees were up in the series, but the Cardinals fought back and took game six to tie. It came down to the final game, and as it turned out, the final pitch.

The Yankees trailed 3-2 in the ninth. With two out, Ruth walked. If he could score, the Yankees would tie the game. Yankee outfielder Bob Meusel dug in at the plate. Suddenly, Ruth took off, trying to steal second! The throw from home came in fast, hard, and on target. Ruth was out, and so were the Yankees.

Ruth was roundly criticized for the play. It dampened an otherwise great series and a great comeback for the Babe.

The loss only made Ruth and the Yankees more determined for victory in 1927. Ruth had proven to his teammates that he was in control of his life, so no one worried anymore about the way he acted off the field. Although he still liked to have fun and still had an enormous appetite, he knew when to stop and made sure that he was ready to play every day.

And play he did. No one will ever forget Babe Ruth and the 1927 Yankees.

Everything went right. Many people still consider the 1927 Yankees the greatest team in the history of baseball. They had great pitching, great fielding, and great hitting. They didn't just beat other teams, they beat them badly. One reason was the emergence of Lou Gehrig.

The very first time a Yankee scout saw Gehrig playing for Columbia University, he called him "another Ruth." Now in his third season in the major leagues, Gehrig was about to serve notice that the scouting report was accurate. Gehrig hit fourth in the Yankees lineup right behind Ruth. Together, the two Yankees stars formed the greatest slugging duo in the history of baseball. Sportswriters dubbed the Yankee lineup "Murderers' Row."

From the start of the season, Ruth and Gehrig sent shivers down the backs of American League pitchers. It seemed as if one of them hit one or two home runs every day. The Yankees scored runs in bunches. One opposing pitcher admitted, "I would rather pitch a doubleheader against any other club than a single game against the Yankees."

Ruth, in particular, seemed invigorated. Every home run hit by Gehrig seemed to spur Ruth on. After all, he had won the major league home run crown in six of the past eight seasons. He didn't want to lose his title to his own teammate.

By mid-season the Yankees were far ahead in the pennant race. The big question became who would lead the league in home runs — Ruth or Gehrig — and whether either man would break Ruth's existing record of fifty-nine home runs.

Entering September, Ruth led Gehrig by two home runs, 43 to 41. Then, on September 6 in Boston, with both men stuck on 44 homers, Ruth pulled ahead. As the Yankees split a doubleheader, Ruth cracked three home runs, including one observers believed was the longest ever hit at Fenway Park. Then the next day he hit two more, putting him only ten home runs behind the record.

Over the final weeks of the season, fans all over the country kept track of Ruth's home runs. And Ruth, knowing everyone was watching, responded with a remarkable performance.

On September 22 his 56th home run in the ninth inning led the Yankees to their 105th win of the season, tying a mark set by the 1912 Boston Red Sox. As he toured the bases with the game-winning hit, dozens of fans poured onto the field and ran with him around the bases. Some of them tried to take his bat, but Ruth held it high over his head, laughing and dashing between his fans on his way to the plate. The record seemed within his grasp.

But over the next week, Ruth hit only one more homer. With only three games left in the season, the record seemed out of reach. It would take what sportswriters called a "Ruthian" performance to hit sixty home runs. Of course, no one was more "Ruthian" than Babe Ruth himself.

On September 29, Ruth broke loose and cracked two home runs to tie the record. After hitting number fifty-nine he shook Lou Gehrig's hand at home plate and then tipped his hat to the crowd. Even Gehrig, who had stalled at "only" forty-seven home runs, stood in awe of Ruth.

Ruth had two more games to try for number sixty.

The next day, the Yankees and Washington Senators were tied 2–2 in the eighth inning. Although Ruth collected two hits and scored both Yankees runs, he had yet to belt out home run number sixty.

With one out, Yankee Mark Koenig tripled. Then Ruth stepped to the plate. He took one ball and one strike. Then Tom Zachary threw another pitch.

The ball was low and inside. With the form he had made classic, Ruth swung down on the pitch and then drove it like a golf ball. The drive sailed to right field, curving toward the line. The umpire tracked the ball to make the call as Ruth started a slow dance toward first.

As the ball rattled into the seats, the umpire signaled fair. Then he twirled his arm above his head, the signal that the hit was a home run.

Yankee Stadium exploded with cheers. Ruth ran around the bases slowly and deliberately, making sure he touched each base. The hit gave the Yankees a 4–2 lead. They hung on through the last inning to win the game.

Ruth was mobbed by reporters in the clubhouse. He had a huge grin on his face. Only two years before, many had thought his career was over. Now he had done something no one else had ever done in the history of the game.

"Sixty!" he yelled. "Count 'em, sixty! Let's see someone else do that!" Then a reporter asked him if he thought he would break his own record in 1928. "I don't know and I don't care," he replied with a laugh.

As wonderful as hitting sixty was, Ruth knew that the Yankees needed to win the World Series to make the record truly meaningful. If the Yankees lost the series, everyone would say he had failed.

He needn't have worried. The Pittsburgh Pirates, the National League champions, were a good team built around Paul and Lloyd Waner, a couple of singles hitters. Before the first game Ruth looked at them and quipped, "Why, they're no bigger than a couple of little kids. If I was that size I'd be afraid of getting hurt."

The 1927 Yankees were a machine. They beat the Pirates 5–4 in the first game and 6–2 in the second. In game three, Ruth blasted his first home run of the series, leading his team to an 8–1 victory. He hit another blast in game four to give the Yankees a 3–1 lead, but the Pirates rallied to tie the game 3–3. Then in the ninth New York loaded the bases. The Pirates pitcher uncorked a wild pitch and Yankee outfielder Earle Combs jogged home with the winning run. Combs hadn't broken a sweat, and neither did the Yankees in sweeping the Pirates. For the second time in his Yankee career, Ruth was a world champion.

When the 1928 season began, New York let every other team know that they were still the champs by winning thirty-four of their first forty-two games. Although Ruth didn't break his home run record, he did come close, slamming fifty-four home runs. The Yankees won the pennant once again and prepared to face the Cardinals.

On paper, it looked as if the Cardinals would have the edge over the Yankees. After their quick start, New York didn't really play very well in the last half of the season. Several New York players would miss the World Series with injuries and Ruth was bothered by a sore knee.

But it seems that no one bothered to tell the Yankees that they were considered the underdogs. They surged forward to sweep St. Louis in four straight games. Once again, Babe Ruth was the big story. He ended the series with perhaps the greatest day of his career.

Ruth wasn't exactly invisible in the first three games, though. Although Lou Gehrig gathered the headlines with three long home runs, Ruth collected three hits in game one, two more in game two, and made the play of the game in the third contest, scoring the go-ahead run by dashing home on a ground ball and knocking the ball out of the catcher's glove.

In game four, however, the legendary player turned in a truly legendary performance. Ironically, he started out as the goat, for in the first inning he dropped an easy fly ball. When he came to bat in the fourth inning, St. Louis led 1–0. With one swing — *Boom!* — Ruth tied the game with a home run.

Then St. Louis went up by one. The score was still 2–1 when Ruth came to bat in the seventh inning. With two strikes the St. Louis pitcher tried an illegal quick pitch. The umpire refused to allow it. Ruth then calmly sent the next offering out of the ballpark. As the St. Louis crowd booed, Ruth laughed his way around the bases, waving at them. Gehrig followed with a home run to put the Yankees ahead.

When Ruth next took the field, St. Louis fans booed him. Some threw soda bottles at him. Ruth picked one up, wound up, and pretended to throw it back. Many fans ducked, but others just laughed as Ruth harmlessly tossed the bottle aside. All of a sudden, they were on his side.

Ruth came up once more in the eighth and put

the game away with another home run, his third of the game. But he wasn't done yet.

With two out in the ninth, the Cardinals were down to their last at bat. A St. Louis batter hit a towering fly ball down the line. Ruth took off, running full speed. Fans in the stands threw paper to try to distract him. It didn't work. Still running, Ruth reached into the stands and snagged the ball without breaking stride. He held it over his head, whooping, "There's the ball! The one that says it's all over!"

For the Cardinals, it was. The Yankees were champions again.

Babe Ruth was at his peak. The Yankees had won three straight pennants and two World Series since he'd taken control of his life. Now he was more beloved than ever.

But Babe Ruth was almost thirty-four years old, ancient for a ballplayer. It would soon be time for him to look to the future.

⋆ CHAPTER SEVEN ⋆

1929–1932

The Called Shot?

The last three seasons had been the best of Ruth's career, and the happiest. He was again the greatest player in the game, and the Yankees were the greatest team in baseball. But the next few seasons would not be quite so enjoyable.

In January of 1929, Ruth received some tragic news. Helen Ruth had been killed in a fire. Although they hadn't been together for years, he was still saddened by her loss. He asked the press to respect her privacy. In April, he married Claire Hodgson. It was clear to everyone that Ruth had settled down.

But no ball club can stay on top forever, and in 1929, the Yankees were in transition. Although Ruth and Gehrig still formed a potent combo, New York's pitching staff wasn't as strong. The Yankees were shaken even further by the death of Miller Huggins late in the 1929 season. Although Ruth and Huggins had clashed, after Ruth's 1925 suspension he and the manager had grown close.

All of a sudden, the Philadelphia Athletics were the best team in baseball. Sluggers Jimmie Foxx and Al Simmons were almost as powerful as Gehrig and Ruth, and fireballing pitcher Lefty Grove led a terrific pitching staff. The A's took off in 1929 and didn't look back. Philadelphia won three straight pennants and two world championships.

Still, Ruth remained one of the most dangerous hitters in baseball. As he grew older, he managed to make small adjustments at the plate to adapt to his slowing reflexes, using a lighter bat and standing a bit further away from the plate. In 1929 he became the first man in the history of baseball to hit 500 home runs in his career, and in 1931 he became the first man to hit 600.

But Ruth and the Yankees really wanted another championship. Ruth realized that at age thirty-six his career as a player would soon come to an end. As early as 1929, after Huggins's death, Ruth hoped to be named Yankee manager. But the ball club wasn't confident that he had the self-discipline for the job. Ruth held onto his hope of becoming the manager sometime in the future. He knew that helping the Yankees win another world championship would help.

In 1932 the Yankees were invigorated by the performance of some younger players, such as catcher Bill Dickey and the emergence of pitcher Lefty Gomez. For the first time in three years, the team finally had enough pitching depth to overtake the A's and win the pennant.

At age thirty-seven, few people expected Ruth to be the star of the World Series against the Cubs. Ruth had hit in only forty-one home runs, far fewer than league leader Jimmie Foxx, who was closing in on Ruth's record with fifty-eight. The Babe's legs were giving him trouble, too, and in September he had been hospitalized with stomach trouble. Before the World Series there was even some speculation that Ruth wouldn't be in the Yankees' starting lineup.

When the series began, however, Ruth was in his usual spot in the right field and hitting third in the Yankee lineup. Although Lou Gehrig had a wonderful World Series, hitting over .500 as the Yankees swept Chicago, all the headlines, as usual, went to Babe Ruth. He did something even he found hard to believe — if he even did it at all.

Former Yankee Mark Koenig had joined the Cubs in mid-season and keyed their pennant run. Yet his teammates had voted him only a half-share of the World Series money. His old teammates on the Yankees, particularly Babe Ruth, thought the Cubs were being unfair to Koenig. In the first two games in New York, both teams razzed each other from the bench. Ruth kept calling the Cubs "cheapskates," and the Chicago players gave it right back to him.

When Ruth and the Yankees went to Chicago for game three, Ruth didn't let up. Wrigley Field, the home of the Cubs, was much smaller than Yankee Stadium. During batting practice Ruth hit home run after home run into the stands. He told a reporter, "If I could hit here all the time I'd play for half my salary."

When the game started, the bench jockeying continued. Even Cubs fans got into the act, and Ruth kept up a running conversation with Cubs players and fans. It grew worse after his first at bat against pitcher Charlie Root. Ruth clubbed a pitch into the stand to give the Yankees a 3–0 lead.

But in the fourth inning Ruth gave the Cubs and their supporters something to howl about. He tried to make a shoestring catch and missed the ball. The hit went for a double and the Cubs were able to tie the game 4–4. Cub fans threw paper and lemons at Ruth and hooted him unmercifully.

Ruth was embarrassed, and also a little mad. He stepped to the plate to lead off the fifth inning determined to quiet the crowd.

As he approached the plate he was booed loudly and the Cubs called him all sorts of names. Ruth listened and then cupped his hands over his mouth and yelled back at them.

The fans started booing even louder. Then Ruth stepped into the batter's box.

Pitcher Charlie Root buzzed a pitch over the heart of the plate and Ruth just watched it pass. Then he turned to the Cub bench and held up one finger, as if to say "That's one."

The howling increased. The Cubs and their fans

wanted to see Ruth embarrassed and humiliated by a strikeout.

Root threw two more pitches for balls, and again Ruth didn't take the bat from his shoulder. It appeared as if he wasn't going to swing.

Then Root threw another strike. Ruth again watched it pass like he was just a spectator. Then he looked at the Cubs and held up *two* fingers as if to say "Strike two."

The crowd was roaring at a fever pitch and Cubs were on the dugout steps screaming at Ruth. He stepped out of the box and gestured to them as if he were pushing them away, like he was some kind of colossus they couldn't touch.

He turned to the Cub catcher and said, "It only takes one to hit it." Root yelled something at Ruth and he yelled back, "I'm gonna knock the ball down your throat."

All the while, Ruth was grinning widely. His gamesmanship was driving the Cubs crazy!

Then Ruth gestured again. To some observers it looked as if he gestured to the Cubs bench again. Others thought he waved at Root. But some were convinced he pointed to the center field bleachers as if that's where he intended to hit the next pitch.

Root wound up and threw. This time Ruth was ready. He took a tremendous swing at the pitch.

Boom! The sound of the bat hitting the ball echoed over the park and stilled the crowd. The ball rocketed directly over Root's head on a line and kept rising, growing smaller and smaller. The Cub center fielder ran straight back and then ran out of room as the ball sailed over his head and deep into the stands in center field.

Ruth just watched, and then, as he jogged toward first base, started to laugh. He had a choice comment for each Cub infielder he passed, plus a few things to the Cub bench as he trotted past third to home.

The Cubs were silent. Ruth had spoken in a way no other player in the game could.

On the very next pitch, Lou Gehrig homered, and the Yankees went on to win the game 7–5 to take command of the series. They won big the next day to capture the series.

But that wasn't the end of the story. Everyone at

the park knew that Ruth had held up his fingers before hitting the home run, and everyone knew that he had made some kind of gesture before belting the home run.

One newspaper reporter captured the mood of the moment, if not entirely accurately, by writing that Ruth had pointed to center field before the pitch and then "punched a screaming liner to a spot where no ball had ever been hit before." The blast became known as the "called shot," and soon everyone was saying Ruth had pointed to center field before hitting the home run.

Witnesses were divided about whether he actually did point, but the story seemed like something only Babe Ruth could have done, or would even have dared to do. Ruth himself claimed that he had pointed "but not [to] a specific spot. I just wanted to give that thing a ride out of the park."

Although film footage turned up later that seemed to indicate that Ruth didn't exactly point, that hardly matters. The legend of the "called shot" already had a life of its own. And even if Ruth didn't point, there is no question that he waited for one pitch and then hit that pitch out of the park. The incident put a tremendous exclamation point on his wondrous career.

He had already done things on the baseball field no one had thought possible, and in doing so had somehow evolved from a sad, lost little boy into one of the most beloved figures in sporting history. Even if Babe didn't point as people claimed he did, there was no question in anyone's mind that if anyone in the history of the game could hit a home run at will, it was Babe Ruth. He was bigger than life, a legend.

★ CHAPTER EIGHT ★

1933 –1947

Heading Home

Not even Babe Ruth could play forever, though. Over the next two seasons it became clear that his strength and stamina were ebbing and that his career was winding down. The Yankees finished second each season and Ruth's performance slowly declined. After hitting .301 with 34 home runs in 1933, in 1934 he hit .288 with only 22 home runs.

Yet Ruth was still the most popular player in baseball. If anything, he was even more popular than ever as fans who had grown up with him now took their children to see him.

On occasion, he could still be the most dynamic player in the game. In the first All-Star game ever, played in Chicago in 1933, Ruth — who else? — hit the first home run in All-Star game history.

He still commanded a big salary, but it was now

more than the Yankees felt he was worth. They wanted him to return in 1935, but only as a pinch hitter and at a reduced salary. Ruth knew his career as a player was coming to an end, but he hoped that his time with the Yankees wasn't over. He hadn't given up his dream of becoming the team's manager.

There was just one problem. The Yankees were happy with current manager Joe McCarthy. When Ruth asked if they were thinking about replacing McCarthy and if he had a chance for the job, he was told no. Although his behavior had improved dramatically, the owners worried that he wouldn't be able to command respect from his players. After all, everyone knew that for most of his career he had flouted the rules. "That's all I need to know," said Ruth when told of the club's decision. Sadly, no other team seemed interested in hiring Ruth as manager either.

While his future hung in the balance, in the off-season he traveled to Japan to help popularize baseball in that country. The game had caught on in Japan, and Ruth was greeted like a conquering hero. But when he returned to America in February, he still didn't know if or where he would be playing in 1935.

Then Judge Emil Fuchs, owner of the Boston Braves, approached Jake Ruppert and asked if he would sell the Babe. The Braves were desperate to draw fans. Fuchs offered Ruth the chance to play one more season as well as a position as a team vice president and assistant manager. He even said he would consider making Ruth manager in the near future.

"If he can better himself elsewhere," Ruppert responded to Fuchs's offer, "the Yankees won't stand in his way." He agreed to release Ruth. If Ruth wanted to sign with the Braves he was now free to do so.

Ruth met with Fuchs and agreed to accept the Braves' offer. He opened the season in the Braves outfield before 25,000 freezing fans in Boston. Ruth, now forty years old, was magnificent. He hit a two-run homer and made a diving catch as the Braves won 4–1. Boston fans went crazy.

Then he stopped hitting. Over the next month he got only two more hits and was bothered by a cold. He also found out that his title as team vice president meant nothing and that Braves manager Bill McKechnie had little use for an "assistant manager."

In early May, a frustrated Ruth wanted to retire. But Fuchs talked him into staying with the team through its next road trip. Thousands of fans had already bought tickets to see him play.

Ruth reluctantly agreed. Except for one last day in Pittsburgh, he played terribly. But on that day, he was as good as he had ever been.

In his first at bat he cracked a two-run home run. Then in his next trip to the plate he hit a second home run. After singling in his third time up, Ruth came to bat one last time.

The pitcher was Guy Bush, who had once pitched for the 1932 Cubs. The bases were empty.

Babe Ruth was forty years old. For a ballplayer, he was old and fat. He had already decided he would retire in a few days.

But he still had one great swing left in him. Bush threw and Ruth hit the pitch on the sweet part of the bat. The ball rocketed into the sky until it was just a small speck. Then it dropped down and down, all the way over the double-decked grandstand in right field at Pittsburgh's Forbes Field. It hit the roof of a house across the street, bounced off another rooftop, and rolled to a stop in a nearby lot. Witnesses later said a young boy walking by saw the rolling ball, picked it up, and went on his way, probably wondering where in the world the baseball had come from. The vacant lot was more than six hundred feet from home plate!

Guy Bush later said, "I've never seen a ball hit so hard before or since." No one had ever even hit a ball onto the roof of the grandstand, much less over it. The blast was the 714th of Babe Ruth's career. It was also his last.

After the game, Duffy Lewis, an old Red Sox teammate who worked for the Braves, told Ruth he should quit at the top and never play another game. But Ruth had promised Fuchs he'd finish the road trip. A few days later, in Philadelphia, he struck out in the first inning, then wrenched his knee and had to leave the game. He never played in the major leagues again.

Less than a week later, he told reporters simply, "I'm quitting." He felt the Braves had broken their promises to him. "I'd still like to manage," he added.

But baseball never really found a place for Babe Ruth after retirement. Yet it never forgot him either.

In 1936 the National Baseball Hall of Fame opened in Cooperstown, New York. Only five players in the history of the game — Babe Ruth, Ty Cobb, Walter Johnson, Christy Mathewson, and Honus Wagner — were selected for induction in that first season. A few years later, in 1939, Babe Ruth coached one season for Brooklyn, but when it became clear they didn't intend to make him manager either, Ruth quit again. He spent most of his time with his wife, Claire, playing golf, giving speeches at clinics, and just relaxing.

He returned to Yankee Stadium on July 4, 1939, for Lou Gehrig Day. His old teammate was dying of a degenerative disease called amyotrophic lateral sclerosis, or ALS, now commonly known as Lou Gehrig's disease. On July 4, the Yankees honored Gehrig with his own day. After Gehrig gave a speech in which he referred to himself as "the luckiest man on the face of the earth" for having the opportunity to play baseball, Ruth gave him a big hug. A few years later, Ruth even played himself in a movie based on Gehrig's life.

During World War II, Ruth helped raise hundreds of thousands of dollars for the Red Cross and made many appearances in exhibitions, hitting home runs and making people smile, like he always had.

In April of 1947, baseball commissioner Happy Chandler declared that it was "Babe Ruth Day" all across the country and Ruth was invited to appear at Yankee Stadium again. He'd been sick and was starting to lose weight. Ruth didn't know it yet, but he was dying.

All his old teammates turned out. So did Johnny Sylvester, the young boy he had hit a home run for, who was now well and a grown man, and 58,000 people in Yankee Stadium to whom he had given such joy. Before the game, he spoke to the crowd with a raspy voice:

"The only real game, I think, is baseball," he said. "You have to start from way down at the bottom . . . You've got to let it grow up with you, and if you're successful and try hard enough, you're bound to come out on top." He was speaking about the game of baseball, but he could have been describing his own life.

Ruth made one more appearance at Yankee Stadium a year later on the twenty-fifth anniversary of "the House that Ruth Built." He was too ill to speak but had one last chance to see his old friends and teammates. Two months later, on August 16, 1948, Babe Ruth died.

Yet a figure as legendary as Babe Ruth can never truly die. When he retired from baseball he held virtually every slugging record — most total bases, highest slugging percentage, most extra base hits, and of course, the most home runs, a total of 714. He even led in career strikeouts and walks.

Although those records no longer stand, no player since has ever been loved as much as Babe Ruth. Wherever children gather to play baseball and dream of making the major leagues and hitting home runs, Babe Ruth, the tough kid who grew up to become the greatest slugger in the game, lives in the hearts of each and every one.

Matt Christopher®

Muhammad Ali

Ichiro

Lance Armstrong

Jennifer Capriati

Shaquille O'Neal

Venus and Serena
Williams

Mario Lemieux

Curt Schilling

Yao Ming

Kobe Bryant

Julie Foudy

Jeff Gordon

Ken Griffey Jr.

Mia Hamm

Tony Hawk

Grant Hill

Derek Jeter

Randy Johnson

Michael Jordan

Tara Lipinski

Mark McGwire

Alex Rodriguez

Sammy Sosa

Tiger Woods

The #1 Sports Series for Kids

Read them all!

All available in paperback from Little, Brown and Company